Contents

CPSIA information can be obtained
at www.ICGtesting.com
Printed in the USA
LVHW071807160320
650151LV00005B/4